So, I've got Dyslexia . . . now what?

Understanding what specific learning difficulties mean to you

by
Dr Hannah Mortimer

Illustrations by Robyn Gallow

A QEd Publication

Published in 2010

© Hannah Mortimer

ISBN 978 1 898873 65 5

British Library Cataloguing
A catalogue record for this book is available from the British Library.

Published by QEd Publications, 39 Weeping Cross, Stafford ST17 0DG
Tel: 01785 620364
Fax: 01785 607797
Web site: www.qed.uk.com
Email: orders@qed.uk.com

Printed by Gutenberg Press Ltd, Malta.

Contents

Introduction

Who the book is for

This book is part of a series written either to speak directly to young people (in this case about 7 to 14 years old) about issues affecting them or to help adults provide support to them. The books are written in an accessible and practical style so that a parent, carer, support assistant, teacher or mentor can work with young people through the book or, if able, they can read them for themselves. The other books in the series include *Fireworks: Managing anger in young children*, *Worry Box: Managing anxiety in young children* and *Bullying: Managing fear in young children*. There is also a helpful booklet on going through a statutory assessment of special educational needs (*Taking Part*).

This book focuses on what it means to have a specific learning difficulty or 'dyslexia' – how young people can make sense of what adults are saying about them and how best to help themselves. It can also be used to offer a simplified explanation of dyslexia (and the issues and misconceptions surrounding it) to share with a referrer prior to or following an assessment. The author usually makes this book available with her reports so as to involve the young person fully in the assessment process and any diagnosis.

Why was this book written?

The author found herself regularly working with young people who had found it hard to develop reading, writing, spelling or maths skills and carrying out assessments that sometimes led to a diagnosis of 'specific learning difficulty' or 'dyslexia'. She would find herself working with a child and gathering information, drawing together the findings for parents, carers and teachers in order to negotiate a picture of the child's difficulties and needs and then making suggestions for the way forward.

However, rarely did she have the opportunity to follow this up with the children concerned to make sure that they understood the implications of their needs and what to expect in terms of their support. This was left to those who lived and worked with the children on a daily basis who would often ask her for advice on 'what to tell the child'. This book is one answer to that question. This book will help those involved get a much better understanding of dyslexia and the support they can expect.

Sometimes the word 'dyslexia' is used and sometimes it is not, depending on who has done the assessment. This can be confusing – not least to the children and parents concerned. This book does not focus on whether or not we should use the label of dyslexia (the amount of research papers and articles on the subject suggest that most professionals find the issue confusing too!). Rather, it aims to help young people understand better what having a specific learning difficulty or 'dyslexia' means for *them*.

What causes the difficulty?

The difficulty often runs in families. Over many years, there has been much debate about possible causes and the most effective interventions. In the author's opinion the most constructive approach is to recognise that these difficulties are very *individual* and that what matters most is identifying each child's strengths and weaknesses and teaching to these.

There is much research into children's literacy learning and the causal factors underpinning literacy learning difficulties. While acknowledging that children may have other associated difficulties, the concept of dyslexia usually focuses on reading and spelling. Phonological awareness (how children distinguish and process the sounds contained in words), is regarded as one of the most convincing explanatory elements. There are often visual difficulties and weaknesses in working memory as well. Learners representing a wide range of general ability and intelligence can have dyslexic problems. There is bound to be much more research as we begin to map processing to areas of the brain.

Over the years, professionals have tended to describe dyslexia as a '*specific* learning difficulty' because the difficulty appeared to go far beyond what we might expect from a child's intelligence quotient (or IQ). This is sometimes known as a 'discrepancy' model. This is because it defines dyslexia in terms of a discrepancy between expected literacy levels (based on a child's IQ) and actual levels – if there is a specific gap and if the child has been taught and supported properly, then dyslexia is likely. Nowadays, it has become less important to assess a child's intellectual ability as part of a diagnosis. This is because research suggests that the literacy problems of children who have general learning difficulties are similar to those experienced by children with higher IQs. That is why it is no longer felt necessary to have a full IQ assessment in order to diagnose a literacy difficulty. It is also why many pupils can and should be assessed and supported within schools without the need for specialist outside assessments. Indeed, in the USA, specialist reading intervention depends not on any discrepancy model but on identifying children at risk of reading difficulty, introducing interventions that have been shown to be effective for most children, and then bringing on board more specialist approaches if these are not effective. This is known as the 'Response to Intervention' model or 'RTI'.

It is interesting that the Joint Council of Exam Boards is already ahead of the debate in that it no longer requires Educational Psychologists (EPs) to do IQ tests to show that a pupil has specific learning difficulty. Instead, access arrangements for external examinations such as GCSE/AS/A2 (such as extra time) are given on the basis of the literacy difficulty as assessed by a specialist teacher or EP (standard scores 85 or below where the average would be 100) regardless of IQ. So all pupils can benefit (regardless of whether they have been diagnosed with a specific learning difficulty or dyslexia), as long as the school judges them capable of handling the content to the course and holds up-to-date evidence of need. EPs can still help by flagging up particular processing difficulties that might not have come to light in the classroom and providing more specialist, 'evidence' that you might need to justify access arrangements.

But people like a label!

We all know this – so we have got be clear about our own definition when applying it. Broadly, this book uses the following definition of dyslexia:

> 'Dyslexia is evident when accurate and fluent word reading and/or spelling develops very incompletely or with great difficulty.'
>
> British Psychological Society (1990)

There could be many reasons why a child was not making adequate progress in literacy skills including lack of opportunity, lack of motivation or poor teaching for that particular child's learning style. Therefore you would not usually speak in terms of 'dyslexia' unless appropriate teaching and differentiation had been tried first.

It is important that parents, pupils and professionals see that dyslexia is a wide label and covers all sorts of abilities – it simply means, when translated, a 'difficulty in reading'! Support should hang not on *label* so much as level of *need* – as described in the *Special Educational Needs Code of Practice* (DfES 2001).

Another issue is that a label somehow imply that a child 'cannot help it'. This might suggest to some that they just accept the label as if nothing else can be done about it. On the contrary, it means that we recognise that these children are going to find it hard but that we are there to help. Every single one of us has aspects of our learning that we can do well and aspects we cannot. If they are 'a bit dyslexic' then this is bound to be an issue for children because school-life carries such a high literacy element. The author spends a lot of her time trying to persuade young people that just because they have dyslexia this does not mean that they are 'stupid' – it is simply that they cannot always show their cleverness when working to and from paper. And schools have a lot of paperwork!

What the SEN Code of Practice tells us

The *Special Educational Needs Code of Practice* (2001) recognises that good practice can take many forms and schools are encouraged to adopt a flexible and a graduated response to the special educational needs (SEN) of individual children. This approach recognises that there is a continuum of SEN and, where necessary, brings increasing specialist expertise on board if the child is experiencing continuing difficulties. Once a child's SEN have been identified, the providers should intervene through 'School Action'. This intervention is coordinated by the SEN Coordinator or 'SENCO'. However, each teacher in the school shares the responsibility of intervening to support the child. School Action involves intervening to support the child and writing an individual education plan (IEP) with three or four clear targets that can be regularly reviewed with parents and carers.

When reviewing the child's progress and the help they are receiving, the teacher might decide to seek more specialist approaches through the support of the outside support services. These interventions are known as 'School Action Plus'. School Action Plus is characterised by the involvement of specialists from outside the school, usually through the Local Authority (LA) Support Service. For a very few children, the help provided by School Action Plus will still not be sufficient to ensure satisfactory progress. The school staff, external professionals and parents may then decide to ask the LA to consider carrying out a statutory assessment of the child's SEN, possibly leading to a 'statement of SEN'.

About one in six children might be expected to have SEN at some stage in their school career and some may require special action to be taken at one point in their schooling and then no longer need it at another. Only about two in a hundred pupils go on to receive a statement of SEN and this figure is decreasing as more support becomes delegated to schools – in fact the whole system will be reviewed before long. Each maintained school now has a budget for meeting the SEN of the pupils which should be ear-marked for those children. However, *special support* does not necessarily mean *individual help* and that budget should be used in a flexible way to make sure a child with SEN is included in the curriculum as far as possible and not segregated or excluded. So we can see that receiving support is not a matter of having a *label* (such as 'dyslexia'), it is a mater of *how great the child's needs are and how well they are responding to the interventions planned for them*.

Independent schools

In independent schools (where the author now works), outside professionals such as the educational psychologist, are often brought in at an earlier stage to enable schools to plan their School Action. This is because LA specialists may not be available to the independent school so they cannot access their advice at the 'School Action' stage. The author finds herself assessing and advising on pupils of all abilities within independent schools in order to provide profiles of strengths and weaknesses when the pupil is learning. This helps her, as an educational psychologist, to advise on ways forward and to work with the teachers, parents and pupils to plan individually-designed approaches. This might or might not involve a diagnosis of 'dyslexia' as such – it depends on what seems to be the most effective way forward in each situation.

Dyslexia organisations

Parents and teachers also make use of organisations such as Dyslexia Action or the British Dyslexia Association (see page 50) where they can access EPs or specialist teachers privately. This means that pupils might be returning to school with a lengthy specialist report with the expectation from parents that these recommendations will be put into place. The first step should always be for parents and the school SENCO to discuss the report together so that it can be interpreted in light of what already goes on within the school's own support system. In addition, this book can be used to explain to adults and young people alike what the assessment means and how to interpret the findings.

How are educational psychologists advised to work?

Educational psychologists are teachers who have specialised in how young people learn, develop and behave. They work with pupils, parents and teachers to see whether, together, they can make a difference. They aim to make school progress and life in general go more smoothly and can advise adults on the best ways of helping children.

In the author's experience, there is still a general feeling that a full educational psychology assessment can be helpful in identifying underlying processing strengths and weaknesses and therefore add to the wider picture when planning effective interventions for children with learning difficulties (specific or otherwise) including dyslexia. It is certainly needed for pupils who are severely affected by their difficulties. In many local authorities, educational psychologists work consultatively with teachers and so help in a non-direct way.

Educational psychologists are recommended to work together with teachers and parents/carers to develop approaches and skills so that individual needs can be identified from an early stage allowing teaching to be adjusted to accommodate these needs. This collaborative process identifies those children whose dyslexic difficulties remain severe and persistent and leads to appropriate additional teaching. So our purpose becomes not one of labelling ('is this dyslexia or not?') so much as assessing strengths and weaknesses to enable teachers and parents to provide the best support and interventions. It will always be the case that there will be pupils who continue to struggle with literacy difficulties/dyslexia and others for whom the barriers are mostly removed. The former group will remain on SEN approaches. The latter group will not.

Meeting SEN inclusively

Inclusion is the practice of including all children together in a school. All children participate fully in all the regular routines and activities of the classroom and school day though these might need to be modified to meet individual children's goals and teaching targets. Recent research studies have suggested that small-group approaches for pupils with reading difficulties can be just as effective as one-to-one sessions and are certainly more inclusive. There seem to be certain common features that promote inclusion:

- There is usually careful joint planning. For example, if there is special support for a child, how will it be used? Will the child still have access to the full range of adults, children and learning activities? Will additional support be provided within class as much as possible?

- Staff use of educational labels rather than categories or medical labels (such as 'a child who has a specific learning difficulty' rather than 'a dyslexic').

- School staff provide good role models for the children because of their positive expectations and the way they respect and value the children. Do they ensure that a child with dyslexia is valued for who they are, for their strengths and as 'ideas people' even if they find it hard to communicate their ideas onto paper? Do they look for alternative means of recording and accessing written information?

- Individual approaches are planned which draw on pupils' earlier experiences, set high expectations, and encourage mutual peer support.

- There is a flexible use of support aimed to promote joining in and inclusion rather than to create barriers and exclusion.

In essence, that means providing schools, classrooms and communities which are 'dyslexia-friendly' and which embrace all three teaching and learning styles – looking, listening and doing in a multi-sensory, step by step and positive way.

Who might benefit from using this book?

1) Young people who are in the process of being assessed. Perhaps they have been referred to a specialist learning support teacher or educational psychologist because of a recognised difficulty in developing literacy skills. Some form of diagnosis or recommendations may have been made and those involved would like to involve the young person fully in that process.

2) Parents and carers whose child has dyslexia. Parents or carers might recognise that their child is being significantly affected by a specific learning difficulty and are looking for advice on what they could do to support their child and minimise any negative emotional effects.

3) The book can also serve as a source of basic information for parents, carers and professionals. It is an attempt to become clearer in our thinking so that we can then be clear when speaking with each other and the young people concerned. It attempts to remove some of the mystery surrounding dyslexia and take a pragmatic approach to dealing with it.

4) An outside professional who has assessed and diagnosed a child with a specific learning difficulty or dyslexia might wish to provide this book for the young person alongside the report to school and parents.

'Talk through' approaches

The book use a 'talk through' approach to provide a framework for the adult and child to talk and work together. Alternatively, if their reading skills are up to it, they can be accessed directly by the young person concerned. You might have met this approach before in the other books in this series. The words in the framework are a guide and work best when used flexibly for the individual child, so that each piece of work seems to flow naturally and feel appropriate for your situation. You are encouraged to think creatively as you work together with the child and to adapt or even design your own sessions as they develop. Though much of it is written as an interaction between an adult and child, it is up to the adult to phrase the wording, and adapt it to suit the situation, age and stage of the child.

Though written under the title of 'dyslexia', the whole book can be flexibly adapted to cover any other of the 'D' word diagnoses sometimes used by professionals such as 'dyscalculia' (a specific number difficulty), 'dyspraxia' (a specific coordination and perceptual organisation difficulty) and 'dysgraphia' (a specific handwriting difficulty).

How to use this book

The following chapters can be used to form a framework for individual sessions between an adult and a young person who has specific learning difficulties or dyslexia. This could be a parent or carer who wishes to support their child following a diagnosis or it could be a teacher, support assistant or support worker in school. Make use of the sessions flexibly, adapting them to suit your particular situation as each child and each pattern of strengths and weaknesses will be different. Not all chapters will apply to all pupils.

In the first chapter, there is a simple explanation of what dyslexia is and what it means. It is quite likely that a young person will have been recently assessed or diagnosed and Chapter 2 describes what that might involve and why. Chapter 3 covers ways of helping and the sorts of interventions that are used. Chapter 4 deals with coloured overlays, tinted spectacles and what is meant by 'visual stress' or 'visual dyslexia'. In Chapter 5 there are ideas for 'brain training', improving memory skills and 'making connections' when thinking and processing. Multi-sensory revision and study skills are covered in Chapter 6, leading into what kinds of arrangements that might be put in place to make taking examinations and further study a little easier (Chapter 7). The book ends with a structured questionnaire in Chapter 8 which allows young people to communicate to the adults in their life what dyslexia means *to them*. This means that they can be more fully included in how their needs are being met. At the end of the book is a resources section including references, helpful books and useful contacts.

| Chapter 1 | Dyslexia – what does it mean? |

First things first

Something brought you to the stage where an adult is sitting down with you to talk about 'specific learning difficulties' or 'dyslexia'. Perhaps you have recently gone through an assessment and your parents have been sent a report saying that you have real difficulties which everyone needs to understand better. Perhaps your teachers have worked out that you find it genuinely difficult to write things down onto paper or to read quickly. Tell your own story here – your helper will write down your words for you if you prefer.

My story – why I am here today

It's only words

Some teachers and specialists talk of 'specific learning difficulties' – this is probably the wording used if you have been assessed and diagnosed within your school. Some (and especially specialists from outside the school such as educational psychologists or those in dyslexia centres) use words like 'dyslexia', 'dyspraxia', 'dysgraphia' or 'dyscalculia'.

Some speak more simply of reading difficulties, spelling difficulties, coordination difficulties, writing difficulties or number difficulties. Others prefer to speak of 'needs' – for example they say that someone has 'literacy needs' or 'numeracy needs', simply meaning that you need more support in either reading/spelling/writing/understanding what you read (literacy) or maths (numeracy). In the end, it's all only words and there will be a lot of overlap. What really matters is the fact that someone has decided that you have genuine difficulties in learning and need more support and understanding so that you can do your best.

Words that have been used to describe my learning difficulties	What I think these words mean

Dyslexia

You can't do a magic test and tell immediately that someone has dyslexia. It's not like an illness that you've either 'got' or 'not got'. It certainly isn't catching – though, because it's to do with thinking and learning in a particular way, it often runs in families. Stop to think of anyone else in your family who might be a weak speller, who doesn't enjoy reading or who has been diagnosed as dyslexic. Do some research and ask around if you need to – you might be surprised!

There are many famous people linked with dyslexia – Leonardo da Vinci, Tom Cruise, Steve Redgrave, Richard Branson, Orlando Bloom and even Albert Einstein are just a few that can be listed.

Other members of my family who might be a bit dyslexic too

Dyslexia means 'difficulty in reading' but if you think about it, that means most children under five would be described as dyslexic and that can't be so. So what we do is look at whether you have been given the *chance* to learn to read first. If you've had all the usual teaching and practise, had just the same opportunities as everyone else – including the usual extra help that all children get in class, worked reasonably hard at it – and if you *still* find reading and writing difficult, then you might be assessed to see if you are dyslexic.

So it is always best to wait a while before getting an assessment to see whether you might be a 'late starter' and catch up with the usual approaches. We can sometimes spot that you might be 'at risk' of being dyslexic early on and plan ways of helping you, but the actual diagnosis tends to arrive after you have been in school a little while. Does this make sense?

Think of your own situation – when did you first begin to find reading and writing difficult? At this stage your teacher probably gave you some extra help in class – perhaps extra reading practice or breaking things down to make them easier for you (this is called 'differentiation'). Can you remember this and was it helpful? Some children feel that they were left to struggle. What was it like for you?

I first began to feel that learning was difficult when . . .

This is what happened next

Other 'D' words

Sometimes people are diagnosed with other kinds of specific learning difficulties. 'Dyspraxia', 'Developmental Dyspraxia' or 'Developmental Coordination Disorder' (DCD) are words sometimes used to describe a difficulty in coordination. They are used in different ways by different professionals such as occupational therapists, physiotherapists and educational psychologists. They usually cover a difficulty in coordinating what your eye sees with what your body does. There is often a bit of clumsiness, you might be poor at games or technology, you might find it pretty impossible to write neatly (even when you try), you might be poorly organised, you might find it hard to make and keep friends and you might find it hard to make sense of what you see, hear and do.

'Dyscalculia' is sometimes used for people who find it very hard to make sense of how numbers work together in maths. This is more than just being weak in maths since there are usually some short-term memory difficulties and a problem in putting numbers in the right order ('sequencing').

'Dysgraphia' is sometimes used by professionals when handwriting skills do not develop despite all the usual kinds of extra help.

Sometimes the term 'complex specific learning difficulties' is used because you have bits of your learning that seem to fit more than one of these conditions – not surprising because there is a lot of overlap. Many of the ways in which you can be helped overlap and so you could easily adapt this book to cover these other conditions as well. Perhaps your helper can encourage you to look any of these terms up on the internet.

Does dyslexia, or any of these others, go away?

It all depends how seriously you are affected and what is done to help. Most people would say that, with the right help and support, your skills will improve greatly – you will improve your reading, spelling, writing or your maths. Perhaps you will get to the point where you no longer need extra support.

However, you might always find these more difficult to do than usual and you might have to concentrate more than usual to get them right. So there isn't an excuse to say, 'I can't do it because I've got dyslexia' – it means that you deserve help and support and probably need to work harder than usual . . . sorry!

The important thing is that teachers and parents should understand that you have to work harder than usual to get it right and they should support you as you do so. You might find that you always need to read or write more slowly than most others because it is hard to read, write and think at the same time. This is one of the reasons why people with specific learning difficulties or dyslexia are often given extra time during tests and exams. Dyslexic adults tend to rely heavily on using a computer when writing, tend to read and write slowly and rely on a good secretary or helper to proof-read for them.

Have I got special educational needs?

Well it depends. Just being 'a bit dyslexic' doesn't mean that you have special educational needs or 'SEN' since lots of people are dyslexic. But if you are really affected by it so that you need help in class which is different or extra to the usual, then you have SEN.

There is something called the *SEN Code of Practice* which tells teachers to put you on 'School Action' if you need approaches which are extra or different to usual. This means that you should have an 'individual education plan' or IEP with a few targets that you are working toward and listing the help you will receive. There should also be a regular meeting with your parents to talk about your IEP and your progress. If you are not already involved in these meetings, ask your teacher whether you can attend too – after all, it is your learning difficulties they are talking about. There is a form below to help you plan your involvement.

Contribution to my IEP Review   Name: _____

The best thing that happened at school this term was:

_____

The worst thing that happened at school this term was:

_____

These were my targets for this term	How well have I done?
1) _____	1) _____
2) _____	2) _____
3) _____	3) _____
4) _____	4) _____

I need more help to do these things: _____

_____

These are things that worry me: _____

_____

This is what I'd like to work on next: _____

_____

Signed: _____   Date: _____

The person who arranges all this in school is called the Special Educational Needs Coordinator or SENCO – sometimes called the Inclusion Coordinator or Learning Support Coordinator. Your helper should be able to tell you who this is.

In our school/college, the SENCO is: _____

If your teachers need advice from an outside professional in order to help you best and if this advice forms part of your IEP, then this is known as School Action Plus.

If you need far more help than is available in the school system, then just a few children go on to have a 'Statutory Assessment' and perhaps a 'Statement' of SEN. These are the children who might need classroom assistance all of the time or even to attend a specialist school for specific learning difficulties where different teaching methods are used.

Talk to your helper about how your needs are being met at the moment.

How my needs are being met	Tick box
I am not receiving SEN assistance at the moment	
My teachers give me a bit of extra help in class	
School Action	
School Action Plus the outside professional that I see is: _____	
I am having a Statutory Assessment	
I have a Statement of SEN	

What causes dyslexia?

This is the million-dollar question. There is still a lot of discussion about it and more research is needed. At the root of most dyslexia is a difficulty in linking letters and sounds – that is why teaching methods which involve phonics (teaching about letter sounds) is usually so helpful.

We know that dyslexic difficulties can run in families so it looks as if they are linked to particular ways in which their brains work. We know that people can be a 'bit' dyslexic and what is important is assessing how greatly you are affected.

We also know that, for some people, there are visual difficulties (see Chapter 6) or a history of early language difficulties. We also see that people with dyslexia often have problems with left and right, with deciding which hand to use most or with getting information in the right order (sequencing) – but so do many people without dyslexia.

Each person's dyslexia will be slightly different and it is all very complex. That is why *your* assessment is so important, since it finds out about your unique pattern of strengths and weaknesses. We will think about this some more in the next chapter.

| **Chapter 2** | **The assessment** |

Perhaps you have already been through an assessment of your specific learning difficulties or perhaps you are about to. In this chapter, we will discuss what this is all about.

Try not to see assessment as being 'tested' in some way – try to see it as 'finding out' – finding out about how *you* happen to learn and remember things best. Assessment should never be simply about labelling ('Have I got dyslexia or not?'), but about finding out about your strengths and weaknesses so that everyone can do the best things to support you. When you think about assessment in that way, you can understand that it should be going on all the time – in your classroom with your regular teachers, with the learning support teacher or SENCO and sometimes with an outside professional such as an educational psychologist.

Within the classroom

Even before you are given School Support, your teachers should be keeping a record of how easily you learn and planning how to help you make progress. State schools follow a national curriculum which gives teachers a map to follow. Pupils are assessed from time to time on SATs (Standard Assessment Tests), but there are also regular records kept and reports made to your parents on progress. Many children who have mild learning difficulties (or who are 'just a bit dyslexic') can be supported in this way. In fact, if only all schools would plan approaches which are 'dyslexia-friendly' (that means using methods which break tasks down and teach using a mixture of looking, listening and doing), then fewer children would have reading difficulties.

A learning support assessment

If your teachers are concerned about your progress and want to find out how to help you more, they usually talk to the SENCO or Learning Support teacher who works for the school. This person might spend some time with you on a one-to-one basis to find out where you need help. They will also talk to your teachers to find out how you are doing in class and also talk with your parents or carers.

To begin with, they will probably look at your reading and spelling.

- Often this involves showing you lists of words on their own and asking you to read them. They start very easy and they always get much harder. This makes sense because they need to stretch you as far as you can go to see how far you have progressed. Everyone gets them wrong at the end – that's meant to happen.

- You might be asked to read words which do not make sense at all. These are called 'nonsense' words. This time you will not be able to use your general cleverness to guess because none of the words is real. This tests your ability to scan the words carefully and remember how different strings of letters make different sounds.

- You will probably be given whole passages of words to read. This allows the teacher to see how smoothly you read, how well you can make sense of what you are reading and how quickly you normally read. Try not to be dismayed if you are asked to read out loud – the teacher has got to hear where any difficulties lie.

- Sometimes you will be shown letters or words made up from different sounds just to see how well your 'phonics' are coming on – this means how well you understand how written letters link to their sounds.

- Sometimes a 'screening test' is used to see how likely it is that you might have a dyslexic difficulty. Because these screening tests have been administered to many children, it is possible to look at your pattern of scores and establish whether you show a similar pattern to those who have been diagnosed as having 'dyslexia'. The test can be used to tell teachers how likely it is that your difficulties are linked to dyslexia.

  For example, there is strong evidence that many dyslexic children are slower than normal to name pictures, especially when there is a whole series of them. Children who have dyslexic difficulties also tend to be more clumsy than usual for their age. They tend to read, write and copy less accurately and more slowly than usual and to have weaknesses in making sense of word sounds. There might be weaknesses in memory – such as finding it hard to remember strings of numbers or, worse still, to remember them backwards.

  There is considerable evidence that dyslexic people find it hard to read nonsense words, even if they have made good progress on ordinary reading. Dyslexic people often have areas of considerable strength, such as in creativity and there might be a test to see whether this applies to you (in fact, you sometimes see advertisements for 'dyslexic architects' because they can often 'think outside the box').

- The teacher might also wish to look at your handwriting and how easily you can copy or write ideas down onto paper. Try to use your usual handwriting and write at the same speed as normal.

- Dyslexia can sometimes affect maths – especially remembering times tables, remembering how to do calculations and working things out in your head. So you might be asked to do some maths as well.

- Sometimes this kind of assessment involves a little bit of teaching too so that the teacher can see how quickly you can pick things up when different teaching methods are used. Part of this will involve working out your 'learning style' – you can do this for yourself on page 39.

The educational psychology assessment

Occasionally you will also meet an educational psychologist. Perhaps this person will come to visit you in school or perhaps you will go to a dyslexia centre for your assessment. Each assessment will be different depending on who you see and what you need. Here is one example from the author so that you can get a good idea about the kinds of work covered. Talk to your helper about how it might compare to your own experience.

An example of the assessment process

Typically, a SENCO would contact me first to say that they would like me to work with you – perhaps because they feel you have dyslexic difficulties and they want to make sure you get all the help you need. Sometimes parents contact me direct – perhaps because they are not sure whether or not there is a learning difficulty and they wish to make sure. However, since these assessments concern learning, I try to persuade school and home to share the information and work together to help you.

By this time, your teachers should already have collected quite a bit of information about how you are learning and I ask them to send this to me. You might have been on an IEP already and again I ask to see these so I can see what has already been done. They will also have contacted your parents and carers to share their concerns and get permission for you to see me. Parents often send in background information before the assessment – especially information about your development, any family patterns of difficulty and whether your hearing and vision has been tested.

Then comes the day of the assessment. I would come into school to see you and you would be expecting my visit. Educational psychologists are teachers who have specialised in how young people learn, develop and behave. They work with pupils, parents and teachers to see whether, together, they can make a difference. They aim to make school progress and life in general go more smoothly and can advise adults on the best ways of helping children. We are not medical doctors or psychiatrists and we become involved in all kinds of problem-solving and not only when things go wrong. If you are still quite young, you may have been told that you will receive a friendly visitor in school who will be doing all kinds of puzzles to find out about how you learn. Most pupils really enjoy the assessment which takes the form of various puzzles and enjoyable challenges.

I might visit the classroom first and observe how the class works – but your friends would not know that I was there because of you. I would make time to talk with your teachers or with the SENCO to find out more. I would also arrange for us to work together where we could work quietly and not be disturbed – usually in a Learning Support room at school. The one-to-one assessment usually takes from one-and-a-half to two hours. If you visited a dyslexia centre it would usually take longer. The time tends to go quickly because you would probably be enjoying yourself and finding it all very interesting. I would let you know how things were going as we worked and hatch some ideas for helping at the end before sharing these with your teachers and parents.

What would I actually do with you? I might try an intelligence test – not because it matters how intelligent you are (since being intelligent means that you are good at doing intelligence tests) but because this also involves looking at how your thinking and remembering works. Some of us find it easiest to think, reason, remember and work things out using words and language. Others are really good at thinking and working things out using spaces and shapes. This is sometimes called your 'verbal intelligence' and your 'non-verbal intelligence'. It is important for your teachers to know this so that they can match your strengths to how they teach you. Most intelligence tests also have a section on how quickly you deal with information – this is sometimes known as your 'speed of processing' and is important to know about in case you need extra time in exams. Finally, they assess your 'working memory' – how easily you can hang on to what you have just seen or heard long enough to deal with it and make sense of it. This area is often weak for pupils who have dyslexic difficulties. Think of it a bit like a short-term memory – you might be brilliant at remembering what happened on your last holiday, but find it much harder to remember instructions, do mental maths or remember what you have just read.

Sometimes pupils come to me telling me that they are 'thick' (these are their words, not mine). The intelligence test can be helpful since it gives them evidence that they are certainly not – it's simply that their reading and writing does not flow smoothly for them. Realising this can make a huge difference to your general confidence and how you see yourself. In fact, this was why the words 'specific learning difficulty' were first used – they meant that your reading, writing and spelling skills were specifically weak for your intelligence – despite being clever enough, you just couldn't show this when working to or from paper. Nowadays we realise that people who haven't learnt to read or write well usually need the same kind of help whatever their level of intelligence so IQ tests are not always used.

Next I would look at your reading, writing and spelling, using the same kind of tests as the Learning Support teachers and which you have already read about. We do these again because it is important to establish that you were not just having a 'bad day' and that there really are difficulties. If maths were a problem, I would look at that area as well. We might also do some memory tests to see whether you remember best when you look at information or when you hear it. We would also talk about how you are feeling about things and the kind of help you think you need. All of this would be written up in a report to be shared with your parents or carers and also the SENCO. The SENCO would then take the recommendations and plan approaches that would be more helpful in school, talking to your teachers and parents in order to do this.

Talk to your helper – how does this compare to your own situation?

About my assessment . . .

Chapter 3	Ways to help

Help from your regular teachers

Sometimes, after the assessment, it may be decided that you have 'learning difficulties' or 'special educational needs'. This is simply another way of saying that you need help in school that is extra or different to the usual. Another way of putting this is that you need learning support . . . somehow that sounds a bit better, doesn't it?

Learning support doesn't have to happen outside the classroom. All your teachers should be made aware of your strengths and weaknesses so that they can break things done for you, make sure you understand and provide work at a level you can manage. Sometimes you might simply need more time to copy things down or some extra help to get your planner sorted out. It is the SENCO's job to make sure that all your teachers know how to help you in the best way. So, if you feel that it is not happening, talk to your parents or to your SENCO. Your helper might be able to assist you with this.

Helping me in class	
What is most difficult for me in class?	
What sort of help do I need?	
Do my teachers understand this?	
Do I need to talk to someone about this?	
Who will I talk to?	
What will I say?	

Extra tuition

Sometimes they might feel that you need some extra tuition – either one-to-one or in a small group. Depending on who has done the assessment, this might be at a dyslexia centre, in school or perhaps even at home.

These tutors should be specialist in teaching children who have specific learning difficulties and will probably follow a special programme with you which teaches you all about phonics (how letters and sounds link together in words) and other reading and writing skills. They will probably teach you in a different way to what you are used to, with plenty of practical activities and games so that you learn by looking, listening and doing – this is called multi-sensory teaching. It always works best when you do the same kinds of things in class, when your tutor and SENCO work together to help you. Otherwise, you might learn how to read and spell with your tutor, but forget it all when it comes to doing this in class or in your homework.

Help from home

It might be that your parents or carers are already helping you by taking you through this book together. You are also likely to find that you need more help with homework and in organising yourself when working at home. Your assessment should have helped them understand what you need a little better. They might also realise that you find things difficult at home as well as school – perhaps because you find it hard to remember instructions or to organise yourself for the school day. The SENCO should be able to provide ideas for helping them to help you. Above all, you will probably need extra support for any homework.

You probably need to work somewhere away from distractions and you might need help to read what you have to do and 'get your head around' it. Perhaps they can help by breaking the task down into smaller steps so that it all seems more manageable. Perhaps they can proof-read what you have read to help you become more accurate. Try not to see this as nagging (they are simply your secretaries!).

If your homework seems to be taking you forever to finish, ask your parents or carers to write a note in your homework diary to explain how long it took and how much help you needed. This should help your teacher set the right level of work for you. Again, talk to the SENCO if this is not working for you. You can see how very important it is that you keep your homework diary up to date and make sure you understand what is involved.

Helping me at home What is most difficult for me at home (e.g. in homework)?	
What sort of help do I need from my parents/carers?	

Helping yourself

Improving your reading fluency

We know that the more reading you do the more easily you will be able to read – just like any other skill. So once you begin to feel more confident – practise, practise, practise.

Look for books which are at the right level for you, but also try to read *anything* – pamphlets, comics, instruction manuals, packaging – anything to help your brain make the connections more smoothly. If you can't understand anything, go back and look again. Read really slowly if you need to – it should speed up a bit with practice. Convince yourself that you can 'crack' the words.

If you find that you much prefer listening to audio books than reading them, try to get hold of books and tapes that go together and follow the text while you listen – even that helps you to develop the right scanning skills. Your local library or SENCO should be able to help.

Improving your reading comprehension

Have you been told that your 'reading comprehension' is weak? What does this actually mean for you? It might be because you have to read very slowly, working out what each word says, word by word. While you are busy doing this, it is hard for you to hold on to the general meaning of the passage at the same time. Some people with dyslexia overcome this by reading very slowly, others by reading a passage or examination question more than once in order to 'get their head round' what it means. That is one of the reasons why they need extra time during written exams.

Sometimes weak reading comprehension is about not understanding the language or the words (the vocabulary) of what you are reading. Unless you tell other people this, they won't be able to understand what is going on.

So what would you say is the reason for you – is it that you can't read what something says or that, even when you can read it, you don't understand it?

This will help you tease apart whether you need more support for your dyslexia and reading difficulty or whether you need to improve your vocabulary and language skills, perhaps through extra help with English.

Ways to improve comprehension

 If you can't understand what a word means, don't skim over it, ask someone . . . either straight away or save it for your teacher/tutor/parent later. Aim to collect a new word every day!

 Work with others – either making the most of group work at school or doing homework with a work-mate. Let your partner do the reading and you contribute to the ideas. It's best to discuss this with your teachers first.

Use a mind map to represent the general ideas of the passage you have read afterwards (see page 42).

 Try to sum up in your own words what you have just read.

 Arrange for a parent/friend to ask you questions about what you have read.

 Photocopy the text (perhaps onto larger or coloured paper if this helps you to read it better) then use a highlighter to outline the main points.

 Ask a parent or friend to read through a passage to you first - some people find that they can understand it much better that way. Then read it yourself so that you already have a gist of the meaning in your head the second time through. Some pupils have a reader during examinations as well if they are severely affected by their dyslexia.

 Work somewhere where you can read out loud and listen to yourself. Stop and re-run if what you hear yourself saying does not make sense. Some pupils even do their examinations in this way, working in a separate room!

Ways to improve your writing

Perhaps you have found that teachers and parents nag you about scruffy handwriting. Unfortunately it does matter because people need to be able to read it. You have to admit that it is quite hard to read the following:

> He usually wears bright clothes. He
> sits at a desk covered in fan mail. His
> helpers are Keith Chegwin, Sara green and
> Crow and the children in the store. In the
> morning he has in celebrities. His brilliant
> programme starts at 9.00 am and finishes
> at 12 o'clock

When you begin to sit exams, the examiners will not be used to your writing and might find it hard to see what you have learned. So you might find yourself having to go right back to the beginning to learn how to form each letter correctly and join them up.

Try to be patient – what you are doing is teaching your hand how to make the right movements all over again, and the more you practise the easier it gets. Try setting up a large whiteboard at home and making huge letters with thick pen. As the movements begin to feel more natural, start writing smaller onto paper. Your helper might be able to practise this with you now.

People might also have said that you hold your pen funnily or press too hard. This matters because, when you have to write longer pieces, your hand might cramp and tire. So ask your SENCO which pens or grips will work best for you if this hasn't already been done. You can also try writing through layers of paper and carbon paper. See whether you can write lightly so that it only comes through two or three sheets of paper.

Computers can help

Above all, get working on your typing skills. If you are lucky enough to be offered touch-typing lessons and if these seem to work for you (they don't for everyone) then take advantage of this. Talk to your teacher or SENCO about typing longer stories or pieces of work in your homework or for projects in class. Do all your coursework on a computer for GCSE. If you find that this works much better than handwriting for longer pieces of writing, then you can even be assessed later to see if you could use a word-processor for external exams such as GCSE. To qualify, you have to be using it regularly at school, you have to be reasonably fast and your writing needs to be very weak. The Spell-check facility is really helpful, not just because it helps you spell better, but because you will need to look carefully at lists of words and choose the right one. However, you will not be allowed to use it during exams.

Computers are really helpful in other ways too. Your SENCO or tutor might have recommended programs to help you learn new skills, such as *Word Shark* or *Number Shark* (see page 52). There is also a helpful website for you to use at home on www.nessy.co.uk . These use a game-like approach which helps you to look, listen and do things. However, you yourself must do a little extra thinking in order to remember the skills you have learned and apply them to your actual work in class – only you can make this link.

Eating well

There is some research that eating properly and drinking plenty of water also helps your brain to work better. In fact, some foods (like two squares of plain dark chocolate a day) work wonders for improving memory. Taking Omega-3 oil appears to really help some people with dyslexia and dyspraxia, so it is worth trying. Do it properly if you are going to try – in other words, take the right dose and do it for at least three months. We also know that eating regularly and healthily, avoiding highly processed foods and artificial additives, helps people learn better. Do you think there is anything you need to work on in order to help yourself more? If so, draw up a target and spend the next month seeing if you can begin to change things.

```
┌─────────────────────────────────────────────────────────────┐
│                 My target for helping myself                 │
│                                                              │
│  Start date: _____        Target date: _____ │
│                                                              │
│                                                              │
│  This is what I will do:  _____ │
│                                                              │
│  _____ │
│                                                              │
│  _____ │
│                                                              │
│                                                              │
│  This is who will help me and what they will do: _____ │
│                                                              │
│  _____ │
│                                                              │
│  _____ │
│                                                              │
│                                                              │
│  This is how I will celebrate if I stick to my target over this time: │
│                                                              │
│  _____ │
│                                                              │
│  _____ │
│                                                              │
└─────────────────────────────────────────────────────────────┘
```

Eyes, brains and things

You can also help yourself by:

- making sure that you can see clearly and telling people if you cannot (Chapter 4);
- exercising your brain so that connections are made more easily (Chapter 5);
- working out the best study and revision style for you (Chapter 6).

Chapter 4	Coloured overlays and tinted glasses

Have you noticed anyone using a coloured overlay or wearing tinted glasses? Perhaps someone has suggested that you try these yourself? Have you wondered what that's all about?

It seems that a lot of people find that, when they try to read, the words do not stay still on the page and this makes it even harder to read them clearly. In fact, all sorts of people find this . . . not just those with dyslexia, though it is more common for those with reading difficulties. This is sometimes known as 'visual dyslexia' though the more accepted word nowadays is 'visual stress'. This is because you don't have to be dyslexic to be affected. However, if you do have visual stress it is bound to make reading harder for you and therefore make you less keen to practise your reading. So it makes sense to find out if you are affected.

Do you have visual stress?

Here is a simple questionnaire to help you find out.

Do words appear to move about when you try to read them?	
Does reading often give you a headache?	
Do the words look blurry (even if you have been checked by an optician and found not to need specs)?	
Does the page look too bright – almost as if the background is brighter than the words themselves?	
Do you eyes start to run and ache after you have been reading for a while?	

If you think you might have visual stress, then the first step would be to have an eye check at your local optician. If you have reading difficulties, you really need to have this done regularly (every year).

It may be that you are short-sighted or long-sighted and you need glasses or contact lenses. However, the optician might find there is nothing wrong and you might feel a bit confused about this, given that words on the page still move around for you! This is the stage you might wish to ask for a more specialist check for 'visual stress'.

Coloured lens prescribers

These are professionals who work out whether you have visual stress (there is a list of them on www.s4clp.org). Because it is known that coloured overlays (sheets of colour-tinted plastic) or lenses can help to correct the condition, they use special apparatus to work out the best colour for *you*.

It is no good just trying out a colour and seeing if it helps on a particular day – the assessment will help to provide *exactly the right tint for your eyes*. It is very individual and many children say that the overlays work 'like magic' for them. They often find that they do not need them forever since their eyes become more used to scanning fluently and smoothly (perhaps because they find it easier to practise their reading!)

Colour overlays and tinted specs do not work for everyone but don't give up unless you have had your particular colour scientifically measured first. This involves showing you patterns under different lights and seeing how this changes your vision.

You might be wondering how on earth they work. It's all rather complicated – visual stress is thought to be related either to how light patterns (such as the patterns of the strokes within letters and words) interfere to cause confusion in the nerve pathways . . . or how the nerve cells themselves operate and switch each other on and off. The coloured overlay changes the light frequency and alters this effect. It is interesting that people who have visual stress also tend to have more migraines in their families. Is this true for you?

Reading rulers

Do you find that you often lose your place when reading? Perhaps you rely on a card or a finger to keep your place. Sometimes reading rulers are recommended. Have you tried these? They come in colours and have a window through which you can see the phrase to read. They help you keep your place and also help to overcome visual stress. You might be able to try them out if your school has sets (see page 52). They come in many different shades. See if there is one that works for you. However, having exactly the right colour recommended for you by a Coloured Lens Prescriber might be more useful if you find that the ruler doesn't really work.

Meares-Irlen Syndrome

If you have been given this label, don't worry. A syndrome is simply a collection of ways in which you might be affected by a condition. The word is sometimes used instead of visual stress because Mears and Irlen were the first people to find out about the condition. It does not mean that you've got a serious illness – it simply means that you definitely show visual stress and need to have something done about it (such as an individually prescribed colour-overlay or specs).

Chapter 5 | Brain training

Some people find that doing certain exercises (described below) can improve thinking skills because the activity increases the brain messages crossing from one side of the brain to the other.

Many sporting activities do this anyway and some people find that these help their thinking skills as well as their body fitness. Research on all this is not clear but it is worth trying some 'Brain Gym' exercises and seeing whether they make it easier for you to concentrate. There is an excellent book of exercises called *The Learning Gym* by Erich Ballinger available through www.optimal-learning.net.

Here are some ideas to get you going, written for younger children, but easy to adapt depending on what age you are. There are suggestions for possible storylines if you are younger so that it feels less like an exercise and more like playing around.

Double Cross

What to do

Raise one knee and bring the opposite hand across to touch it. Repeat for the other hand and knee. Do this several times.

Possible storyline

You're a superhero trying to save the world from Dr. Zolomain, but he has taken over your mind and is controlling your body.

These exercises are thought to be helpful for:

- spatial awareness (understanding spaces and shapes);
- the ability to distinguish between right and left;
- awareness of personal space and physical boundaries (where your body is in space);
- whole-body coordination;
- binocular vision (helping the eyes work together as a team).

This exercise provides cross lateral stimulation just as a crawling motion does. Some children with developmental dyspraxia are said to have missed out on the benefits of that stage as babies. This exercise can help them make the necessary connections that should help to improve their coordination.

Double High

What to do

Write your name or draw a doodle in the air with your dominant hand. Then use the other hand and try writing your name in mirror writing/doodle *at the same time*. This is hard and takes some practice but people find it to be a really helpful exercise.

Possible storyline

Plan an adventure in 'Mirror World'!

This exercise is thought to be helpful for:

- helping your eyes work together as a team;
- coordinating your eye and hand movements;
- helping to establish handedness, right or left;
- helping you learn about direction so that it becomes easier to identify letters and numbers.

Some children with dyslexia find this exercise particularly helpful. You can follow it up in real life by encouraging mirror doodling on a white board.

Pieces of Eight

What to do

Hold a thumb in the air and focus your eyes on your thumbnail. Keep your eyes on your thumb and trace an infinity sign (a figure of eight on its side) in front of you with a large circle to the right and one to the left. Your helper can show you how. Swap hands and repeat, then try both together.

Possible storyline

. . .and now the Great Wizard seems to be controlling us . . . Oh no! He's trying to hypnotise us with our own thumbs!! (In a hypnotic voice) 'watch the thumb, watch the thumb' . . . no, this is not working . . . now he's trying the other thumb. Here we go again!

This exercise is thought to be helpful for:

- helping your eyes work as a team;
- stopping the confusion of letters like b/d;
- encouraging you to recognise and distinguish letters and numbers;
- helping you write with less stress;
- improving balance and coordination

Some children with dyslexia find this exercise particularly helpful. It is sometimes known as the 'Lazy 8s' exercise and is an easy way to learn to smoothly cross the visual midline that connects left and right visual fields.

Fold-ins

What to do

Hold your arms out straight in front and cross them over. Turn palms inwards so they face each other and clasp fingers. Bring hands towards the body and up, finishing under your chin. Again, your helper can show you how.

Possible storyline

Make this a ritual signal for a world-saving secret society. How will members meeting for the first time recognise that you are one of the 'goodies'?

This exercise is thought to be helpful for:

- helping coordination;
- keeping hands out of mischief (stopping you fiddling or 'piggling');
- calming you when things are getting rather excited

Some children with attention difficulties find this exercise particularly helpful. It calms and contains them and gives them a clear boundary, keeping them out of trouble.

Deep Breathing

What to do

Sit straight and breathe in from deep in your stomach. Your helper can do it with you as you breathe slowly, steadily and in time with each other.

Possible storyline

Use this as part of your wind-down at the end of your exercises. You could also include this action in an underwater adventure perhaps.

This exercise is thought to be helpful for:

*   relaxation;
*   thinking clearly in exams and tests;
*   calming yourself after a period of activity or excitement.

Some children who get anxious about their work find this exercise particularly helpful. It also helps all children with their learning since it allows them to take in plenty of oxygen to fuel their brains. Don't forget the other fuel for thinking and learning over the day – plenty of water to drink!

Chapter 6   Revision and study skills

This chapter is for those of you who have to revise and study for exams and tests.

Have you been in a situation where you have had to learn and revise a lot of material ready for a test or exam? Perhaps you have found it particularly difficult? How do you revise at the moment?

My revision method

Does it work well?

We are all different and remember and learn best in different ways. Everyone would find it useful to discover what their particular learning style is so that they can use the best revision approach for *them*. When you have dyslexia or a specific learning difficulty, this is even more important than usual because it might be that some parts of your memory are working better than others. Spend some time with your helper working out your particular style.

Learning styles

We all learn differently and it makes sense to work out what kind of learner *you* are. Some of us learn best by *looking*, some by *listening* or some by *doing*. Most of us learn in a combination of all these ways and the best teachers usually use all three methods.

Think of the teachers you work well for – how to they teach you? Is there a lot of listening involved? Do you have to watch the board a lot? Do they get you talking to each other or trying practical activities out? The three learning styles are usually known as **visual**, **auditory** and **kinaesthetic**.

Below is a Learning Styles checklist. Try using this to discover your most successful learning style. Simply circle the letter if the sentence applies to you and see whether one learning style seems to work better for you than any other.

Learning Styles Checklist	V/A/K
Reading When presented with an illustrated book, do you enjoy looking through the pictures?	V
Do you enjoy listening to stories rather than reading them?	A
Are you good at explaining stories?	A
Do you prefer listening to story tapes?	A
Does lots of close print and small letters confuse you?	A
Do you fiddle a lot when reading?	K
Are you good at using expression and tone of voice?	A
Writing Do you think your handwriting is neat and nice to look at?	K
Do you tend to think out loud when writing?	A
Do you enjoy writing in your own words?	A & K
Do you like to add illustrations, diagrams and decoration?	V & K
Do you spell best by saying the letter sounds out loud?	A

Learning Styles Checklist	V/A/K
Writing continued	
Do you spell best when you write the words first and then check?	V
Do you enjoy working in diagrams, mind maps and pictures?	K
Mathematics	
Do you need to work through examples with an adult first in order to understand what you need to do?	K
Can you learn by simply watching a friend work through an example?	V
Do you like to talk yourself through examples out loud?	A
Can you follow instructions in Maths if a teacher simply *tells* you what to do?	A
Do you prefer to use counters or fingers when adding and subtracting?	K
Do you prefer to use a number line or number square?	V
General	
Do you enjoy music making?	A
Do you like to watch others first before joining in with anything new?	V
Do you need instructions repeated?	V
Do you tend to move your arms and hands around when speaking?	K
Have you ever had speech and language difficulties?	V
Would you rather demonstrate something than explain it?	K

Learning Styles Checklist	V/A/K
General continued	
Do you need to look directly at someone speaking in order to understand better?	K
Do you have difficulty remembering unless you make notes?	V & K
Do you daydream a lot during listening activities?	V
Do you prefer to watch an activity rather than get stuck in?	V
Do you enjoy craft and making things?	K
Are you easily distracted by noise?	A
Are you easily distracted by things to look at?	V

Summary of learning style

A – auditory _____ out of 12

V – visual _____ out of 12

K – kinaesthetic _____ out of 12

Now try to find the best revision and study method to suit *your* style. On the following page are a number of suggested methods of studying and revision under each of the learning styles that are worth trying. There is also a useful booklet called *The Great Little Book of Revision and Showing you Know* from Intelligent Minds (details on page 51).

Visual revision methods

 Try making revision notes in different colours so that they are easier to visualise and remember.

 Use highlighters to flag up important information in your notes.

 Draw flow charts and diagrams to represent the information - now try to close your eyes and visualise it.

 Use mind maps in different colours to summarise important information (see the example below).

 Watch DVDs about the topic you are revising.

 Make bullet-points on coloured memory cards.

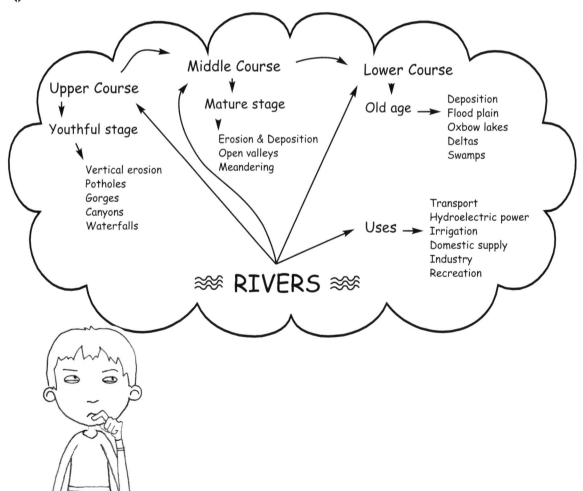

Auditory revision methods

 Read your notes out loud to yourself.

 Record your notes and then listen back to the CD or tape.

 Discuss your notes with a friend.

Sum up the information to a parent or friend.

Kinaesthetic revision methods

 Copy key information down.

 Move about whilst you read your notes to yourself.

 Chant information whilst bouncing a basket ball or bouncing on a trampoline!

 Listen to a recording of your notes whilst doodling – try to make doodles that sum up the information you are listening to.

The best revision method *for me*

Chapter 7	Extra time and stuff

This chapter is all about how you might be helped during tests and exams. Your helper should be able to keep you up to date with what the various regulations say (there are contact details on page 50), since they tend to change a little from year to year.

Here is broadly what you can expect in terms of arrangements to help you manage school tests and external exams as best you can.

Extra time during examinations

If you have been assessed as having a learning difficulty that is likely to affect you during an exam, it is quite likely that additional time might have been recommended for you. Some people with dyslexia find that they need this time to read and re-read the questions, to plan their answers, to get their answers in the right order, to read or write more slowly than usual or to check and double-check their answers. Of course, many people would find this extra time useful so the system has to be fair to everyone. That is why there are quite strict regulations about who can, and who can't, have extra time during important examinations.

The person doing your assessment has to be clear that your particular learning difficulty acts as a barrier to your showing what you know during an examination – and therefore that it wouldn't be fair if you *didn't* have that extra time. Unfortunately you don't get extra time simply for being just a weak speller as very many of us are. As long as the examiner can work out what you are trying to write, poor spelling should not get in the way of your passing exams.

People who are given extra time sometimes take their exams in a separate room from the others which can be useful if you get easily distracted. The usual amount is 25% extra though some have less and some even more, depending on the nature of their difficulty. The extra time is only useful if you learn how to use it and if you have practice in using it during internal school exams first. If you have been granted extra time during exams, talk to your helper about how you need to use that time.

Sometimes people feel embarrassed about taking their extra time. Schools should organise exams so that you do not feel too self-conscious and there are often several of you needing it together.

Extra time during exams

I need extra time during exams because: _____

_____

_____

I will use it in this way: _____

_____

_____

I will be able to practise this when: _____

_____

_____

If you have been assessed as needing extra time before the end of Year 6, this will need reassessing after Year 7 in order to receive extra time for GCSEs.

Other access arrangements

Some people who are severely affected by their dyslexia or specific learning difficulty also need someone to help read the questions and the longer blocks of text to them. Your reading has to be very weak to qualify for this – it is just for those who couldn't possibly read or understand the questions themselves. Having a teacher or friend to read to you should be your normal method in class. By the way, if you use a coloured overlay to help you read, you are allowed to take this into examinations.

Others might need someone to write their answers for them – this is called a 'scribe' or an 'amanuensis'. More common is permission to use a word processor (laptop or computer) during exams – perhaps because you write quicker on a computer or you find it easier to think things through when working on a computer. Unfortunately, you don't get permission to use a computer simply because you are better at this than when handwriting. There has to be a major problem in reading your writing, in your speed of writing or how you get your thoughts down onto paper. You are not allowed to use the spell check facility during exams.

SATs

During Standard Assessment Tests (SATs), many children with learning difficulties are helped by a reader or a scribe for certain papers. It is more difficult to obtain permission for extra time and this is assessed carefully by the SENCO. It might be that you have been assessed by an outside professional who has found out that you meet the criteria. In GCSEs the situation is reversed – a school can give you additional time if they have the evidence, but have to apply for special permission to give you a reader or a scribe or the use of a word processor.

Going on to university or college

It is worth while showing any professional report to your university or college when you leave school. There is a section to complete when you apply for loans which asks whether you have any specific learning difficulty. Do be honest about this. If you needed extra time and specialist help at school, it is very likely you will need this when the reading and writing becomes more intense during Higher Education depending on your chosen subject. If you are going to apply for special equipment and funding (which you can do if you are significantly affected by your dyslexia), then you will be asked to provide an educational psychology report gathered in the last two years. This is to make sure that the system is fair to everyone.

What of the future?

How will your specific learning difficulty affect you as an adult? It all depends on how seriously you are affected and how much of the right sort of help you have received and taken on board.

Many adults with dyslexia say that they have to read and write more slowly than usual. They take written information away to study rather than try to digest it quickly and in front of others. They rely heavily on computers for writing and planning (who doesn't?) and need a good proof-reader to check their spellings.

They tend to shy away from jobs which are paper-based and often pursue creative and practical careers, or at least make sure that they have good administrative and secretarial support to back them up.

Chapter 8   Letter to my SENCO

Now that you have come to the end of this book, you will have done a great deal of thinking about what your specific learning difficulties mean to you and the kind of help you feel you need. Here is a letter that you and your helper could put together summing it all up.

It is the SENCO's job to coordinate how your needs are met in school and so it would make sense for the SENCO to have a copy. This makes sure that your views are included in the action that the school is taking to help you.

If you and your helper look back through your answers in this book, you will be able to complete the letter. Alternatively, you might like to type out your own version.

Confidential

Dear (name of SENCO) _____

I have been talking about my specific learning difficulties with

(name of helper) _____

Here is what we talked about so that it can be kept with my school records and shared at my next review meeting.

These are the words we used to describe my learning difficulties:

_____

_____

This is how I feel my learning difficulties affect me:

_____

_____

This is the help I am getting at the moment:

_____

_____

This is what I find most difficult in class:

_____

_____

This is the sort of help I would like in class:

_____

_____

This is what I find most difficult about homework/Prep:

_____

_____

This is the sort of help I need for my homework/Prep:

_____

_____

I am planning to do these things to help myself more:

_____

_____

I think my best learning style is:

_____

So I think my best revision method will be:

_____

This is the sort of help I feel I need during exams and tests:

_____

_____

These are the most important things I would like you to tell my teachers, please:

_____

_____

Thank you for helping me.

Signed: (your name) _____   Signed: (your Helper) _____

Date:_____

Useful books, resources and organisations

For official SEN Guidance

British Psychological Society (1990) *Dyslexia, literacy and psychological assessment.* Report of a working party of the Division of Educational and Child Psychology. Leicester: British Psychological Society.

DfES (2001) *The Special Educational Needs Code of Practice* (ref DfES 581/2001)
www.education.gov.uk

Contact your Local Authority Children's Services for local information on inclusion and special needs

For information about access arrangements for GCSE and GCE contact
The Joint Council for Qualifications
Tel: 020 7638 4132
Website www.jcq.org.uk and enter 'Access' in the search

For information about access arrangements for SATs contact
Qualifications Curriculum Development Agency
Tel: 0300 303 3010
www.naa.org.uk/tests

For guidance on the definition of a disability contact
www.direct.gov.uk/en/YoungPeople

Useful organisations

The following organisations provide different levels of support, including information on needs, services, centres, support groups, resources and training.

British Dyslexia Association
Tel: 0845 251 9002
www.bdadyslexia.org.uk

Dyslexia Action
www.dyslexiaaction.org.uk

Dyspraxia Foundation
Tel: 01462 454 986
www.dyspraxiafoundation.org.uk

The Helen Arkell Dyslexia Centre
Tel: 01252 792 400
www.arkellcentre.org.uk

Anything Left-handed Ltd
Tel: 0845 872 3272
www.anythinglefthanded.co.uk

To contact an Educational Psychologist

For Local Authority schools, contact your school SENCO, your local Children's Services or your Local Authority for information about your local educational psychology service and their referral system.

British Psychological Society for a directory of chartered psychologists
Tel: 0116 254 9568
www.bps.org.uk

Association of Child Psychologists in Private Practice
Tel: 07770 804175
www.achippp.org.uk

For an Educational Practice for Independent Schools in Yorkshire and North East area, contact the author Dr Hannah Mortimer, Chartered Educational Psychologist
hannah.mortimer@pillrigg.fsnet.co.uk

Coloured lens information and prescribers
www.s4clp.org
www.irlenuk.com

Useful books

The Great Little Book of Revision and Showing you Know from Intelligent Minds
Tel. 01243 572132
www.trainthebrain.co.uk

The Learning Gym by Erich Ballinger
www.optimal-learning.net

Worry Box: Managing anxiety in young children and
Fireworks: Managing anger in young children by Dr Hannah Mortimer
Tel: 01785 620364
www.qed.uk.com

Working with Children with Specific Learning Difficulties in the Early Years by Dorothy Smith
Tel: 01785 620364
www.qed.uk.com

Helpful software and websites

Word Shark and Number Shark
Tel: 0208 748 5927
www.wordshark.co.uk

The Nessy programs including BrainBooster are really useful at home
Tel: 0117 9239777
www.nessy.co.uk .

Crossbow Education (for reading rulers)
Tel: 0845 269 7272
www.crossboweducation.com

www.getrevising.co.uk

www.bbc.co.uk/schools/revision